The Martini

A Postcard Book™ Twenty-eight Classic Cocktails, with Recipes

RUNNING PRESS
PHILADELPHIA · LONDON

© 1998 by Running Press Book Publishers
Photographs © Steve Belkowitz

All rights reserved under the Pan-American
and International Copyright Conventions

Printed in China

*This book may not be reproduced in whole or in part, in any form
or by any means, electronic or mechanical, including photocopying,
recording, or by any information storage and retrieval system now
known or hereafter invented, without written permission from the publisher.*

Postcard Book is a trademark of Running Press Book Publishers.

9 8 7 6 5 4 3 2 1
Digit on the right indicates the number of this printing

ISBN 0-7624-0371-3

Designed by Frances J. Soo Ping Chow
Recipes compiled by Gary Regan and Mardee Haidin Regan
Edited by Gena M. Pearson

This book may be ordered by mail from the publisher.
Please add $2.50 for postage and handling. *But try your bookstore first!*

Running Press Book Publishers
125 South Twenty-second Street
Philadelphia, Pennsylvania 19103-4399

Introduction

—◦◦◦—

Widely known as the world's most elegant cocktail, the Martini has been surrounded by an air of sophistication ever since its mysterious invention. One school of thought holds that John D. Rockefeller was the first to partake of this concoction at New York's Knickerbocker Hotel in 1910; others believe that the drink was served to a gold miner as early as 1849 at a bar in Martinez, California. Whatever its origin, the Martini is a truly fabulous cocktail of enduring appeal, with hundreds of variations being served in bars and restaurants around the world.

From the traditional Dry Vodka Martini to more elaborate creations such as the Four Seasons Gotham Martini and the award-winning Copper Illusion Martini, *The Martini* offers twenty-eight recipes you can keep or send to your friends. The recipes are from some of North America's most elegant hotels, finest restaurants, trendiest bars, and swankiest watering holes.

Whether you're a first-time Martini sipper or a seasoned connoisseur, this elegant cocktail companion celebrates a drink that is simply sublime—the King of all Cocktails: the Martini.

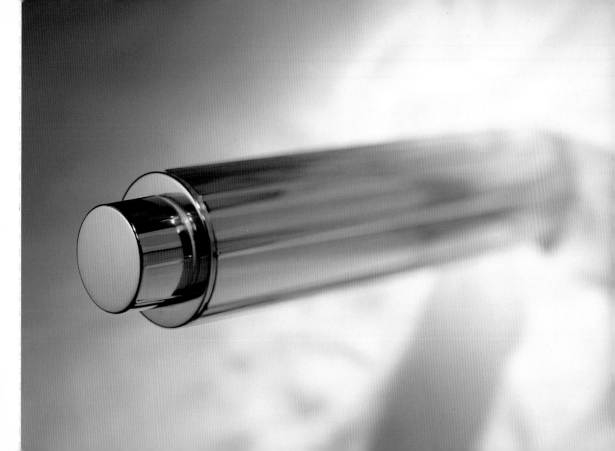

James Bond's Vesper Martini

3 ounces gin
1 ounce Russian vodka
½ Lillet Blanc
1 thin lemon twist, for garnish

Shake and strain. Garnish with lemon.

The Martini, A Postcard Book™
©1998 by Running Press Book Publishers
Photograph © Steve Belkowitz

The Almond Joy Martini

created by "Diamond" Dave Kiernan,
Johnny Love's, San Francisco

Chocolate syrup, for rimming the glass
sliced almonds, for garnish
1¼ ounces Tanqueray Sterling vodka
¼ ounce Malibu rum
¼ ounce amaretto liqueur

Pour enough chocolate syrup into a shallow bowl to fill it about ½ inch deep. Invert the rim of a frozen Martini glass in the chocolate syrup so that the interior and exterior of the rim are coated with the syrup. Remove the glass and hold it over the bowl so any extra syrup can drip back into the bowl.

Stick several of the thinly sliced almonds to the inside of the glass. Pour the vodka and rum into a mixing glass half filled with ice cubes.

Stir and strain into the prepared glass. Pour the amaretto down the side of the glass so that it rests in the center of the bottom of the glass.

The Martini, A Postcard Book™
©1998 by Running Press Book Publishers
Photograph © Steve Belkowitz

The Cherries Jubilee Martini

from the Purple Martini, Denver

3 ounces Ketel One vodka
splash of amaretto liqueur
1 maraschino cherry, for garnish

Shake and strain. Garnish with cherry.

The Martini, A Postcard Book™
©1998 by Running Press Book Publishers
Photograph © Steve Belkowitz

The Finlandia Blue Moon Martini

created by Kevin Crafts for Finlandia Vodka's Fashion Martini series

1½ ounces Finlandia vodka
1½ ounces Finlandia Pineapple vodka
½ ounce blue curacao liqueur
1 orange twist, for garnish

Stir and strain. Garnish with orange twist.

The Martini, A Postcard Book™
©1998 by Running Press Book Publishers
Photograph © Steve Belkowitz

The French Martini

from the Morton's of Chicago Martini Club

3 ounces Tanqueray gin
dash of Pernod
1 lemon twist, for garnish

Stir and strain. Garnish with lemon twist.

The Martini, A Postcard Book™
©1998 by Running Press Book Publishers
Photograph © Steve Belkowitz

The Italian Martini

from the Cruise Room in the Oxford Hotel, Denver

3 ounces vodka
splash of Campari
1 orange slice, for garnish
1 lemon slice, for garnish

Stir and strain. Garnish with orange and lemon slices.

The Martini, A Postcard Book™
©1998 by Running Press Book Publishers
Photograph © Steve Belkowitz

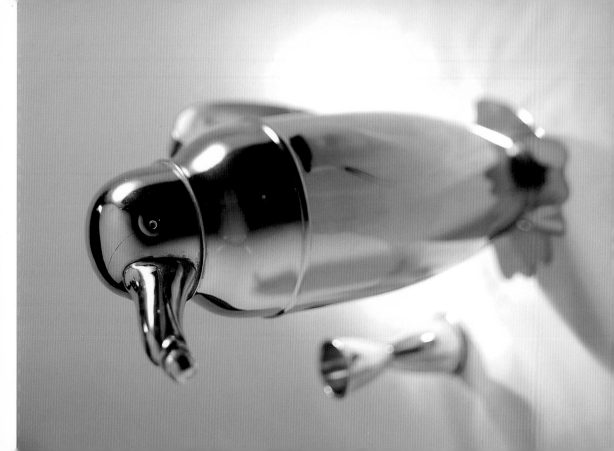

The Ivory Coast Martini

from the Purple Martini, Denver

3 ounces gin
splash of white créme de cacao
splash of dry vermouth

Stir and strain.

Manhattan Cocktail

from the *Bar-Tenders' Guide* by Jerry Thomas

(The order of the ingredients has been altered.)
3 dashes Boker's bitters
2 dashes Curacao or Maraschino
1 pony of rye whiskey
1 wine-glass of vermouth
2 small lumps of ice

Shake and strain into a claret glass.

The Markfish Martini

created by Gary Regan and Mardee Haidin Regan

2½ ounces Stolichnaya Kafya vodka
¼ ounce Stolichnaya Zinamon vodka
1 short cinnamon stick, for garnish

Stir and strain. Garnish with cinnamon stick.

The Martini, A Postcard Book™
©1998 by Running Press Book Publishers
Photograph © Steve Belkowitz

The Melon Martini

from the Cruise Room in the Oxford Hotel, Denver

3 ounces Absolut vodka
1 ounce Midori Melon liqueur
1 orange slice, for garnish

Stir and strain. Garnish with orange slice.

The Olympic Gold Martini

Winner of Seattle's 1993 Martini Challenge
created by Michael R. Vezzoni, The Four Seasons Hotel, Seattle

1 ounce Bombay Sapphire gin
1½ ounces Absolut citron vodka
⅓ ounce (1 teaspoon) Canton Original Ginger liqueur
⅙ ounce (½ teaspoon) Martell Cordon Bleu cognac
1 lemon twist, for garnish

Stir together for 40 revolutions. Strain into an ice-cold glass.
Garnish with lemon twist.

The Martini, A Postcard Book™
©1998 by Running Press Book Publishers
Photograph © Steve Belkowitz

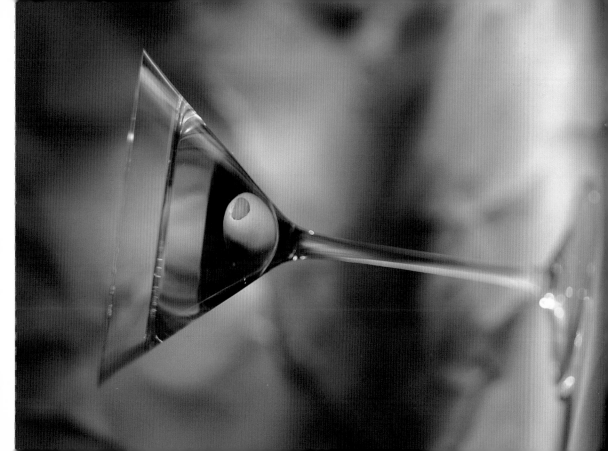

The Orange Mandarine Martini

from the Purple Martini, Denver

3 ounces Stolichnaya Orange vodka
splash of Grand Marnier
1 orange slice, for garnish

Stir and strain. Garnish with orange slice.

The Martini, A Postcard Book™
©1998 by Running Press Book Publishers
Photograph © Steve Belkowitz

The Pear Martini

from the Morton's of Chicago Martini Club

3 ounces Stolichnaya vodka
½ ounce Poire William eau-de-vie

Stir and strain.

The Scotland Yard Martini

from the Cruise Room in the Oxford Hotel, Denver

3 ounces Beefeater gin
splash of scotch
1 lemon twist, for garnish

Stir and strain. Garnish with lemon twist.

The Martini, A Postcard Book™
©1998 by Running Press Book Publishers
Photograph © Steve Belkowitz

La Serre's Tequila Martini

from the Four Seasons Hotel, Toronto

2 ounces Jose Cuervo Gold tequila
½ ounce Cointreau
½ ounce Grand Marnier
1 orange twist, for garnish

Stir and strain into a large "fish bowl" snifter.
Garnish with orange twist.

The Mint Martini

from Boulevard, San Francisco

Colored sugar, for rimming the glass
1½ ounces vodka
splash of green créme de menthe
1 miniature candy can, for garnish

Rim the exterior of a chilled Martini glass with colored sugar. Pour the vodka and
créme de menthe into a mixing glass filled with ice; stir until chilled. Strain into the
prepared glass. Garnish with candy cane.

The Martini, A Postcard Book™
©1998 by Running Press Book Publishers
Photograph © Steve Belkowitz

The Michel Martini

created by Gary Regan and Mardee Haidin Regan

2½ ounces Stolichnaya Vanil vodka
¼ ounce Stolichnaya Zinamon vodka
3 redhots (small, red, heart-shaped candies), for garnish

Stir and strain. Garnish with redhots.

The Martini, A Postcard Book™
©1998 by Running Press Book Publishers
Photograph © Steve Belkowitz

The Gotham Martini

from the Four Seasons Hotel, New York

3 ounces Absolut vodka
½ ounce blackberry brandy
½ ounce black sambuca
3 blackberries, for garnish

Stir and strain. Garnish with blackberries.

Norman's Watermelon Martini

created by Norman Bukofzer, The Ritz-Carlton Hotel, New York

2½ ounces gin
¼ ounce Marie Brizard watermelon liqueur
Juice of 1 lime wedge
1 lemon twist, for garnish

Stir and strain. Garnish with lemon twist.

The Staibilizer Martini

from Villa Christina, Atlanta

3 ounces Tanqueray Sterling vodka
splash of Galliano
splash of Frangelico

Stir and strain.

The Terrace-tini

created by Charles A. Shepherd, River Terrace Yacht Club, Memphis

½ ounce Grand Marnier
4 ounces Bombay Sapphire gin
1 orange slice, for garnish

Pour the Grand Marnier into a well-chilled Martini glass and tilt to coat the interior. Stir the gin over ice until very cold; pour into the prepared glass. Thread orange slice onto a sword pick and use as garnish.

The Martini, A Postcard Book™
©1998 by Running Press Book Publishers
Photograph © Steve Belkowitz

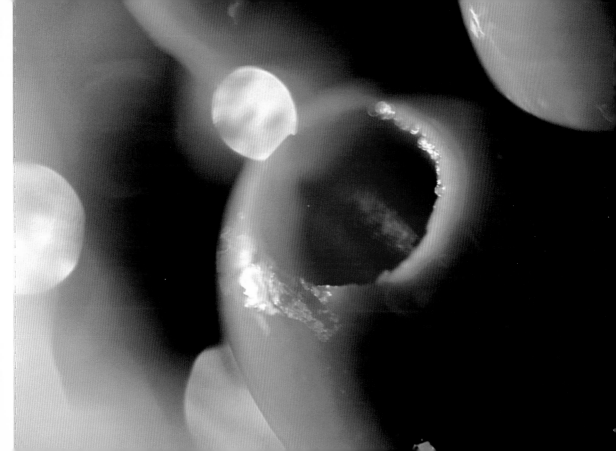

The Valencia Martini

from Pravda, New York

4½ ounces gin or vodka
splash of Dry Sack sherry

Stir and strain.

The Samara Martini

created by Gary Regan and Mardee Haidin Regan

2½ ounces Stolichnaya Kafya vodka
¼ ounce Stolichnaya Razberi vodka
1 fresh raspberry, for garnish

Stir and strain. Garnish with raspberry.

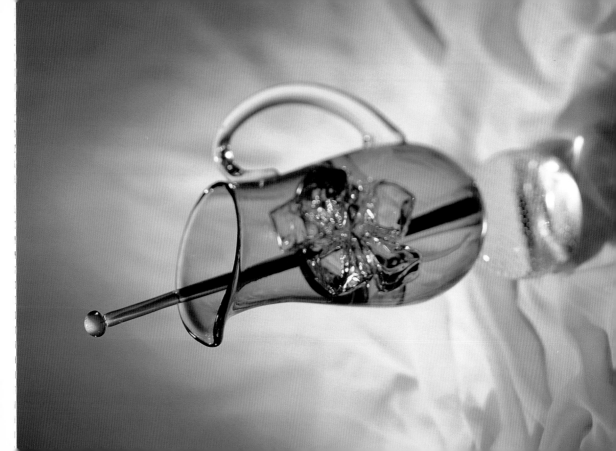

Martini Jo

created by Chef Jean Joho, Brassiere Jo, Chicago

3½ ounces Skyy vodka
½ ounce Lillet Rouge
1 orange twist, for garnish

Shake well with ice and strain into a chilled glass. Rim the glass with orange twist and drop into the drink.

The Martini, A Postcard Book™
©1998 by Running Press Book Publishers
Photograph © Steve Belkowitz

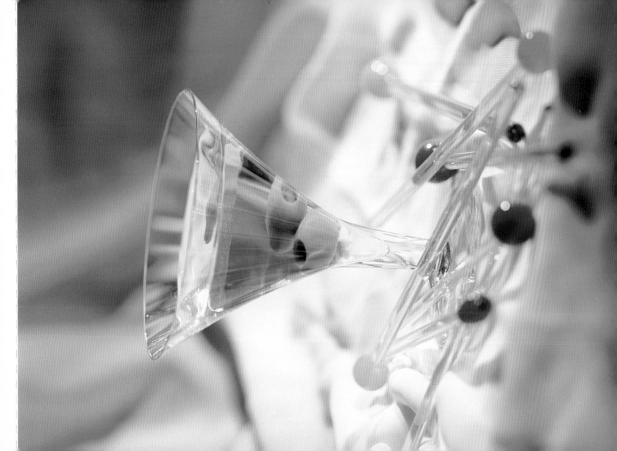

The Mansion Martini

from the Mansion on Turtle Creek, Dallas

splash of tequila
3 ounces Bombay Sapphire gin or Stolichnaya Cristall vodka
2 jalapeño-stuffed olives, for garnish

Rinse the glass with tequila and discard the tequila. Stir the liquor over ice until very cold. Strain into a chilled glass. Garnish with olives.

The Martini, A Postcard Book™
©1998 by Running Press Book Publishers
Photograph © Steve Belkowitz

The Copper Illusion Martini

Winner of Seattle's 1994 Martini Challenge
created by Michael R. Vezzoni, The Four Seasons Hotel, Seattle

2½ ounces Beefeater gin
¼ ounce Campari
¼ ounce Cointreau
1 orange twist, for garnish

Stir together for 40 revolutions. Strain into an ice-cold glass.
Garnish with orange twist.

The Martini, A Postcard Book™
©1998 by Running Press Book Publishers
Photograph © Steve Belkowitz